meals in minutes

make-ahead dinners

RECIPES
Rick Rodgers

PHOTOGRAPHS
Bill Bettencourt

weldon**owen**

contents

FOUNDATION RECIPES

about this book

The secret to making healthy, delicious meals when you are pressed for time is to plan ahead. With only a little advance preparation, you will be able to put home-cooked meals on the table without spending a lot of time in the kitchen. Using quality ingredients from your pantry, Meals in Minutes *Make-Ahead Dinners* will provide you with countless ideas for weeknight meals.

With Meals in Minutes *Make-Ahead Dinners* you'll learn how to make a big batch of delicious Roasted Tomato Sauce to serve over pasta one night, then store it to use for later meals, such as hearty Meatball Sandwiches or Baked Rigatoni with Ricotta and Sausage. Recipes such as Baked Ham with Green Beans will give you enough ham for dinner tonight plus rich Croque Monsieurs and creamy Pappardelle with Ham and Peas. Other recipes, such as Asian Salmon Cakes can be completely prepared and frozen for when you want a healthy, stress-free meal.

foundation
recipes

ziti with arugula pesto & chicken

ARUGULA PESTO

Garlic, 2 cloves

Pine nuts, ½ cup (2½ oz/ 75 g)

Baby arugula (rocket), 5 cups (5 oz/155 g)

Parmesan cheese, ½ cup (2 oz/60 g) freshly grated

Olive oil, 1 cup (8 fl oz/ 250 ml)

Salt and freshly ground pepper

Ziti, 1 lb (500 g)

Unsalted butter, 2 tablespoons

Cooked, shredded chicken, 2 cups (12 oz/375 g), purchased

Cherry tomatoes, ½ lb (250 g), halved

Ricotta salata, 1 cup (4 oz/125 g), crumbled

Parmesan cheese, ¼ cup (1 oz/30 g), freshly grated

SERVES 4–6

makes about 4 cups (32 oz/1 l) pesto total

Instead of making a traditional pesto with basil, use peppery arugula. Use it for this hearty pasta dish, then serve it later in the week as a spicy sauce for fish, or a delicious spread for grilled panini.

1 **Make the pesto**
Bring a large pot of water to a boil over high heat. In a food processor, combine the garlic, pine nuts, arugula, and Parmesan. Pulse to chop. With the machine running, gradually add the oil. Season with 1 teaspoon salt and several grindings of pepper. Reserve ½ cup (4 fl oz/125 ml) of the pesto and store the remaining pesto for future use (see Storage Tip, right).

2 **Cook the pasta**
Add 2 tablespoons salt and the pasta to the boiling water. Cook, stirring occasionally to prevent sticking, until the pasta is al dente, according to the package directions. Drain, reserving about ½ cup (4 fl oz/125 ml) of the cooking water. Return the pasta to the pot.

3 **Finish the pasta**
Meanwhile, in a large frying pan over medium-high heat, melt the butter. Add the chicken and cook, stirring occasionally until heated through, 3–4 minutes. Add the chicken to the cooked pasta, along with the reserved ½ cup arugula pesto, the tomatoes, ricotta salata, and Parmesan. Mix, adding as much of the cooking water as needed to loosen the sauce, season with salt and pepper, and serve.

storage tip

The pesto can be stored in airtight containers in the refrigerator for up to 1 week or in the freezer for up to 1 month. Drizzle olive oil over the surface before covering with the lid to prevent discoloration. Bring the pesto to room temperature and stir before serving.

grilled halibut with arugula pesto

1 Prepare the grill

Prepare a gas or charcoal grill for direct-heat grilling over high heat. Lightly oil the grill rack. Brush the halibut with the oil and season generously with salt and pepper.

2 Grill the halibut and tomatoes

Place the halibut over the cooler area of the grill and the tomatoes over the hotter area of the grill and cover. Grill the halibut and tomatoes, turning once, until the fish looks opaque when pierced with the tip of a knife and the tomatoes are tender, about 10 minutes. Arrange the halibut and tomatoes on a serving platter, top with the arugula pesto, and serve.

Arugula Pesto (page 10), 6 tablespoons (3 fl oz/90 ml), at room temperature

Olive oil, 3 tablespoons

Halibut fillets, 4, about 1½ lb (750 g) total weight

Plum (Roma) tomatoes, 4, halved lengthwise

Salt and freshly ground pepper

SERVES 4

cook's tip

Serve the halibut with roasted new potatoes. To make them, preheat the oven to 400°F (200°C). Halve the potatoes and place on a rimmed baking sheet. Toss with 1 tablespoon olive oil, season with salt and pepper, and roast until crisp and golden, 15–20 minutes.

fontina, ham & pesto panini

Arugula Pesto (page 10),
½ cup (4 fl oz/125 ml),
at room temperature

Country-style white sandwich bread, 8 slices

Fontina cheese, 4 oz (125 g), thinly sliced

Black forest ham, 8 oz (250 g), thinly sliced

Olive oil, 3 tablespoons

SERVES 4

1 Prepare the panini

Spread the pesto on one side of each slice of bread. Place 4 bread slices, pesto sides up, on a work surface. Top each slice with equal amounts of the cheese and ham. Cover with the 4 remaining slices of bread, pesto sides down. Brush the panini on both sides with the oil.

2 Cook the panini

Heat a panini press over medium heat and brush generously with oil. In batches, if necessary, add the sandwiches, then place the weighted lid on top. Reduce the heat to medium-low. Cook until the undersides are golden, about 2 minutes. Turn, weigh the sandwiches down again, and cook until the other sides are golden, about 2 minutes longer. Cut the sandwiches in half and serve.

cook's tip

In place of a panini press,
use a large, heavy grill pan. Heat
the empty pan over medium
heat. Lightly oil the pan, add the
panini, and place a flat lid
or plate on top of the sandwiches
to weight them down. Cook
as directed in Step 2.

pasta with roasted tomato sauce

ROASTED TOMATO SAUCE

Red bell peppers (capsicums), 2, seeded and quartered

Yellow onions, 2, cut into wedges

Plum (Roma) tomatoes, 3 lb (1.5 kg), halved lengthwise and seeded

Garlic, 2 heads, halved crosswise

Olive oil, ¼ cup (2 fl oz/ 60 ml)

Salt and freshly ground pepper

Fresh basil, 1 cup (1½ oz/ 40 g) chopped

Fettuccine, 1 lb (500 g)

SERVES 4

makes about 8 cups (64 fl oz/2 l) sauce total

This flavorful roasted tomato sauce brings new life to traditional marinara. This version yields enough sauce to serve over pasta tonight and use in meatball sandwiches and baked rigatoni later.

1 Roast the vegetables
Preheat the oven to 450°F (230°C). Place the peppers, onions, tomatoes and garlic on two rimmed baking sheets. Toss the vegetables with the oil and season with salt and pepper. Roast the vegetables until tender and golden, about 30 minutes. Let cool until easy to handle.

2 Finish the sauce
Bring a large pot of water to a boil over high heat. Remove and discard the skins from the tomatoes and peppers and transfer the flesh to a bowl. Squeeze the roasted garlic from the cloves into the bowl and add the onions and basil. In a food processor, pulse the vegetable mixture until coarsely chopped. Season with salt and pepper. Reserve 3 cups (24 fl oz/750 ml) of the sauce, and store the remaining sauce for future use (see Storage Tip, right).

3 Cook the pasta
Add 2 tablespoons salt and the pasta to the boiling water. Cook, stirring occasionally to prevent sticking, until the pasta is al dente, according to the package directions. Drain, reserving about ½ cup (4 fl oz/125 ml) of the cooking water. Add the pasta to the sauce and stir to combine. Add as much of the cooking water as needed to loosen the sauce and serve.

storage tip

Let the roasted tomato sauce cool
completely and store in airtight
containers in the refrigerator for
up to 3 days or in the freezer
for up to 3 months. When
freezing, always store in small
portions (3–4 cups/24–32 fl oz/
750 ml–1 l) so that you can
thaw as needed.

cook's tip

You can prepare the meatballs
up to 2 months in advance.
After forming the raw meatballs,
place them on a baking sheet or
other pan and freeze thoroughly,
about 2 hours. Transfer to an
airtight container. Before using,
defrost the meatballs in the
refrigerator overnight.

meatball sandwiches

1 Prepare the meatballs

In a large bowl, combine the bread crumbs and milk and let stand about 5 minutes. Meanwhile, in a large frying pan over medium-high heat, warm the 1 tablespoon oil. Add the onion and garlic and cook, stirring occasionally, until the onion is translucent, about 5 minutes. Let cool slightly and add to the bread crumb mixture. Add the egg, parsley, 1 teaspoon salt, 1/4 teaspoon pepper and the beef to the bowl and mix gently with your hands. Form into 12 meatballs.

2 Cook the meatballs

In a large frying pan over medium heat, pour oil to a depth of 1/2 inch (12 mm). When the oil is hot, add the meatballs. Cook, turning occasionally, until browned on all sides, about 8 minutes. Transfer to a paper towel–lined plate to drain. Discard the oil and place the pan over medium-low heat. Pour the roasted tomato sauce into the pan, stirring and scraping up any browned bits from the pan bottom. Add the meatballs to the pan and cook, covered, until heated through, about 10 minutes.

3 Make the sandwiches

Meanwhile, preheat the oven to 450°F (230°C). Place the open rolls, cut sides up, on a baking sheet. Spread equal amounts of sauce on the bottom half of each roll. Arrange 3 meatballs on each roll and top with equal amounts of mozzarella. Bake until the cheese melts, about 5 minutes. Transfer to plates, spoon the remaining sauce over the sandwiches, and serve.

Roasted Tomato Sauce (page 16), 2 cups (16 fl oz/ 500 ml)

Fresh bread crumbs, 1/2 cup (1 oz/30 g)

Milk, 2 tablespoons

Olive oil, 1 tablespoon, plus more for frying

Yellow onion, 1 small, finely chopped

Garlic, 1 clove, minced

Egg, 1, beaten

Fresh flat-leaf (Italian) parsley, 3 tablespoons chopped

Salt and freshly ground pepper

Ground (minced) beef, 1 1/2 lb (750 g)

Crusty rolls, 4, each about 6 inches (15 cm) long, split lengthwise

Fresh mozzarella cheese, 6 oz (180 g), thinly sliced

SERVES 4

19

baked rigatoni with ricotta & sausage

Roasted Tomato Sauce (page 16), 3 cups (24 fl oz/ 750 ml)

Olive oil, 2 tablespoons

Italian sausage, casings removed, 1 lb (500 g)

Pitted black Mediterranean olives, 1 cup (5 oz/155 g) coarsely chopped

Salt and freshly ground pepper

Rigatoni, 1 lb (500 g)

Ricotta cheese, 1¾ cups (15 oz/470 g)

Parmesan cheese, ¼ cup (1 oz/30 g) freshly grated

SERVES 4–6

1 Prepare the sauce

Preheat the oven to 350°F (180°C) and lightly oil a deep 2½-quart (2.5-l) baking dish. Bring a large pot of water to a boil over high heat. In a large frying pan over medium-high heat, warm the oil. Add the sausage and sauté, breaking up the sausage with a spoon, until browned, about 6 minutes. Drain any excess fat from the pan. Stir in the tomato sauce and olives, season to taste with salt and pepper, and set aside.

2 Cook the pasta

Meanwhile, add 2 tablespoons salt and the pasta to the boiling water. Cook, stirring occasionally to prevent sticking, until the pasta is not quite al dente, about 2 minutes less than the package directions. Drain, rinse under cold running water, and drain again.

3 Bake the pasta

Return the pasta to the cooking pot. Stir in the tomato sauce and ricotta. Spread the pasta and sauce in the prepared dish and sprinkle with the Parmesan. Bake until the surface is golden and bubbly, about 25 minutes. Let cool for 5 minutes and serve.

cook's tip

To complete the menu, toss fresh mixed baby greens with your favorite vinaigrette. Whisk together 1 ½ tablespoons red wine vinegar, 1 minced shallot, and ⅓ cup olive oil. Season the vinaigrette to taste with salt and freshly ground pepper, dress the salad, and serve.

roasted shrimp with romesco

ROMESCO SAUCE

Garlic, 2 cloves

Slivered almonds, 1 cup
(4½ oz/140 g), toasted

**Roasted red bell peppers
(capsicums),** 2 jars (12 oz/
375 g each), drained

Sherry vinegar, 4 teaspoons

Smoked paprika,
2 teaspoons

Olive oil, 6 tablespoons
(3 fl oz/90 ml)

**Salt and freshly ground
pepper**

Large shrimp (prawns), 2 lb
(750 g), peeled and deveined,
tails intact

Olive oil, 1 tablespoon

SERVES 4

makes about 2½ cups
(20 fl oz/625 ml) romesco
sauce total

Romesco sauce is a unique Spanish condiment
with a peppery, nutty flavor. In the recipes that follow
you will find it adds zest to roasted vegetables and
makes the perfect marinade for grilled pork chops.

1 **Make the romesco sauce**
Preheat the oven to 450°F (230°C). In a food processor,
chop the garlic finely. Add the almonds and pulse until finely
chopped. Add the roasted peppers, vinegar, and paprika and
process until smooth. With the machine running, gradually
add the 6 tablespoons oil. Season with salt and pepper. Reserve
½ cup (4 fl oz/125 ml) of the sauce and store the remainder
for future use (see Storage Tip, right).

2 **Roast the shrimp**
On a large baking sheet, toss the shrimp with the
1 tablespoon oil and season generously with salt and pepper.
Roast, tossing occasionally, until the shrimp are opaque
throughout, 4–6 minutes. Spoon the romesco sauce into small
bowls for dipping. Divide the shrimp among individual plates
and serve with the sauce.

storage tip

The romesco sauce can be stored in airtight containers in the refrigerator for up to 1 month. Drizzle olive oil over the surface before covering with the lid. Bring to room temperature and stir well before serving.

cook's tip

Romesco sauce is usually served
on the side as a condiment, but
it makes a great seasoning paste
as well. Whisk with 2 tablespoons
of olive oil to loosen the sauce
before using on meat or poultry.

roasted vegetables with romesco

1 Roast the potatoes

Preheat the oven to 450°F (230°C). In a small saucepan over medium-low heat, warm the oil and garlic until the garlic is golden, about 5 minutes. Remove from the heat and discard the garlic. On a large, rimmed baking sheet, toss the potatoes with 1 tablespoon of the garlic oil and roast for 10 minutes.

2 Add the vegetables

In a large bowl, toss the zucchini, eggplant, bell pepper, and onion with the remaining garlic oil and add to the baking sheet with the potatoes. Roast, turning occasionally, until the vegetables are tender, about 20–30 minutes. Season with salt and pepper. Transfer the vegetables to a platter, top with the romesco sauce, and serve.

Romesco Sauce (page 22), 1 cup (8 fl oz/250 ml)

Olive oil, ¼ cup (2 fl oz/ 60 ml)

Garlic, 2 cloves, smashed

Small red potatoes, 1 lb (500 g), halved

Zucchini (courgettes), 2 large, halved lengthwise and cut into 1-inch (2.5-cm) pieces

Asian eggplant (slender aubergines), 2, cut into 1-inch (2.5-cm) pieces

Red bell pepper (capsicum), 1 large, seeded and cut into 1½-inch (4-cm) pieces

Red onion, 1, cut into thick rings

Salt and freshly ground pepper

SERVES 4–6

grilled pork chops with romesco

Romesco Sauce (page 22),
½ cup (4 fl oz/125 ml)

Boneless, center-cut pork chops, 4, each about
1 inch (3 cm) thick

Salt and freshly ground pepper

Olive oil, 6 tablespoons
(3 fl oz/90 ml)

Yukon gold potatoes,
1½ lb (750 g), scrubbed

Sherry vinegar, 1 tablespoon

Green (spring) onions,
3, chopped

SERVES 4

1 Marinate the pork chops

Season the pork chops with salt. In a shallow dish, whisk the romesco with 1 tablespoon of the oil. Add the chops, toss to coat, and let stand at room temperature for up to 1 hour.

2 Make the potato salad

While the pork is marinating, bring a saucepan of water to a boil over high heat. Add 1 tablespoon salt and the potatoes. Cook until the potatoes are tender when pierced, about 25 minutes. Drain, rinse under cold running water, and let cool slightly. In a large bowl, whisk together the remaining 5 tablespoons oil and the vinegar. Halve and slice the potatoes and transfer to the bowl. Add the green (spring) onions and mix gently. Season with salt and pepper and set aside.

3 Grill the pork chops

Prepare a gas or charcoal grill for indirect grilling over high heat. Lightly oil the grill grate. Place the pork chops on the cooler area of the grill and cover. Let cook for 5 minutes. Turn and grill until the pork chops feel firm when pressed in the center, about 5 minutes longer. Serve the pork chops with the potato salad.

cook's tip

Fresh chopped vegetables such as red bell peppers (capsicums) and celery make flavorful additions to the potato salad. It can be prepared up to 1 day in advance. Cover and store in the refrigerator. Let the potato salad come to room temperature before serving.

cheese & rosemary stuffed focaccia

FOCACCIA DOUGH

Olive oil, ¼ cup (2 fl oz/ 60 ml), plus more as needed

All-purpose flour, 3½ cups (17½ oz/545 g), plus more as needed

Active dry yeast, 5 teaspoons (2 packages)

Salt, 1½ teaspoons

Warm water (110°F/43°C), 1¼ cups (10 fl oz/310 ml)

Teleme jack or Monterey jack cheese, 4 oz (125 g), thinly sliced

Fresh rosemary, 2 teaspoons chopped

Freshly ground pepper

SERVES 8

makes 2 flatbreads total

With this dough, you can make an assortment of savory meals. Here, the dough is used for cheese-stuffed focaccia, but it can also be used to make muffaletta sandwiches or deep-dish pizza.

1 Make the dough

Lightly oil two 8-inch (20-cm) square pans and a large bowl. In a food processor, combine the flour, yeast, and salt and pulse to blend. Add the warm water and ¼ cup oil and pulse until the dough comes together. Let the dough rise in the oil-coated bowl until doubled in bulk, about 1¼ hours. Divide the dough in half.

2 Shape the dough

Pat and stretch one dough half into one of the prepared pans. Brush the top with oil, cover tightly with plastic wrap and then aluminum foil, and freeze for another use (see Storage Tip, right). Divide the other dough half into 2 pieces. Pat and stretch one portion into the remaining pan. Top with the cheese and rosemary, leaving a ½-inch (12-mm) border. On a lightly floured work surface, pat and stretch the remaining piece of dough into an 8-inch square. Place in the pan, covering the cheese and rosemary, and pinch the dough layers together. Cover with a damp kitchen towel and let rise again for 1 hour.

3 Bake the dough

Preheat the oven to 400°F (200°C). Brush the dough with oil, dimple with your fingertips, and bake until golden brown, about 25 minutes. Transfer to a wire rack and let cool briefly in the pan. Cut into wedges or squares and serve warm.

storage tip

The focaccia dough, shaped
into square 8-inch (20-cm)
or round 9-inch (23-cm) pans,
can be frozen for up to
1 month. To thaw, place in the
refrigerator overnight or let
stand at room temperature,
covered with the plastic
wrap until the dough looks
puffy, about 3 hours.

cook's tip

This olive salad is extremely
versatile. Serve it on sliced,
toasted, country bread as a quick
bruschetta or as a spread for
other sandwiches.

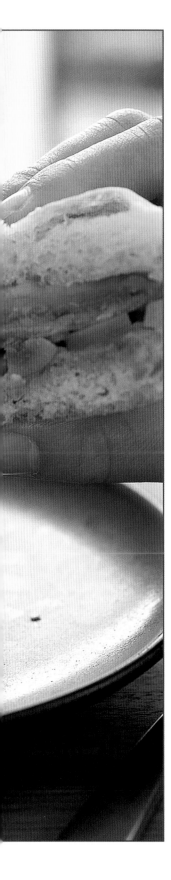

warm muffaletta sandwiches

1 Bake the dough
Preheat the oven to 400°F (200°C). Uncover the dough and dimple the top of the dough with your fingertips. Brush with oil and sprinkle with sesame seeds, if using. Bake until the focaccia is golden brown, about 30 minutes. Remove from the pan and let cool on a wire rack.

2 Make the olive salad
Meanwhile, mix together the garlic, olives, celery, 2 tablespoons oil, vinegar, and red pepper flakes. Let stand at room temperature to blend the flavors.

3 Toast the sandwiches
Preheat the broiler (grill). Cut the focaccia into 4 equal squares and cut each square in half crosswise, making 8 slices total. Spread the bottom 4 slices with the olive salad, top with the salami, ham, and provolone, and top with the remaining focaccia slices. Place the sandwiches on a baking sheet. Broil (grill) until the cheese melts and the focaccia is golden brown, about 2 minutes. Transfer the sandwiches to a cutting board, cut in half, and serve.

Focaccia Dough (page 28), One 8-inch (20-cm) square, at cool room temperature

Olive oil, 2 tablespoons, plus more for brushing

Sesame seeds, 1 teaspoon (optional)

Garlic, 1 small clove, minced

Pitted green olives, ½ cup (3 oz/90 g) coarsely chopped

Celery, 1 stalk, coarsely chopped

Red wine vinegar, 1½ teaspoons

Red pepper flakes, ⅛ teaspoon

Genoa salami, 4 oz (125 g), sliced

Black Forest ham, 4 oz (125 g), sliced

Provolone cheese, 5 oz (155 g), sliced

SERVES 4

deep-dish vegetable pizza

Focaccia Dough (page 28),
One 8-inch (20-cm) square,
at cool room temperature

Olive oil, 1 tablespoon, plus
more for brushing

Button mushrooms, ¼ lb
(125 g), thinly sliced

Zucchini (courgette),
1 large, halved lengthwise
and thinly sliced

Red onion, 1 small, halved
and thinly sliced

Marinara sauce, 1½ cups
(12 fl oz/375 ml), purchased

Fresh mozzarella cheese,
½ lb (250 g), thickly sliced

Parmesan cheese, ¼ cup
(1 oz/30 g) freshly grated

Fresh basil, 3 tablespoons
chopped

SERVES 2–4

1 **Shape the dough**
Preheat the oven to 400°F (200°C). Pat the dough up the sides of the pan. Cover with plastic wrap and let stand until the dough is spongy, about 30 minutes.

2 **Prepare the topping**
Meanwhile, in a large frying pan over medium heat, warm the 1 tablespoon oil. Add the mushrooms, zucchini, and onion, and cook until the onion is tender and the mushrooms have released their liquid, about 5 minutes. Remove from the heat and let cool slightly.

3 **Bake the pizza**
Spread the marinara sauce on the bottom of the dough, leaving a ½-inch (12-mm) border. Top with the mozzarella slices and the vegetables and sprinkle with the Parmesan. Brush the exposed dough with oil. Bake until the underside of the dough is golden brown, about 25 minutes. Transfer to a cutting board. Sprinkle with the basil, cut into pieces, and serve.

cook's tip

A mixture of cheese such
as creamy fontina or sharp feta
would work well with this
pizza. You can also mix up the
vegetables and add sliced
sun-dried tomatoes or chopped
broccoli florets.

mushroom
tart

CREAM CHEESE DOUGH

All-purpose (plain) flour,
2 cups (10 oz/315 g), plus
more for rolling out the dough

Salt, 1 teaspoon

Unsalted butter, 1 cup
(8 oz/250 g), chilled, cut into
cubes

Cream cheese, 8 oz (250 g),
at room temperature, cut into
cubes

Unsalted butter,
2 tablespoons

Mixed fresh mushrooms,
such as cremini and stemmed
shiitake, 1½ lb (750 g) halved
or quartered

Shallot, 1 large, chopped

**Crème fraîche or heavy
(double) cream,** ½ cup
(4 fl oz/125 ml)

Fresh oregano, 1 teaspoon
chopped

**Salt and freshly ground
pepper**

SERVES 6

Makes 1 tart and 2 pastry
dough disks total

A food processor makes flaky pastry dough in a flash.
This recipe yields enough dough for two recipes,
such as this savory mushroom tart and the spinach
tartlets or chocolate turnovers that follow.

1 Make the dough
In a food processor, combine the flour and salt and pulse
briefly to mix. Add the butter and cream cheese and pulse
until the mixture just starts to come together. Transfer to a work
surface, divide into 2 equal portions, and press each portion
into a flat disk. Set 1 disk aside and wrap the other disk in plastic
wrap for future use (see Storage Tip, right).

2 Bake the tart shell
Preheat the oven to 400°F (200°C). On a floured work
surface, roll out the dough into a 12-inch (30-cm) round.
Fit into a 9-inch (23-cm) round tart pan and trim the dough
to a ½-inch (12-mm) overhang. Fold the overhang over itself
and pinch to create a sturdy edge. Pierce the dough all over with
a fork. Freeze for 15 minutes. Bake until the edges are lightly
golden, about 15 minutes. Let cool on a wire rack.

3 Make the filling and finish the tart
In a large frying pan over medium heat, melt the butter.
Add the mushrooms and shallot and cook, stirring occasionally,
until lightly browned, 8–10 minutes. Add the crème fraîche
and oregano, season with salt and pepper and stir to combine.
Spread the mushroom mixture in the shell. Bake until the
crust is golden, about 15 minutes. Let cool briefly on a wire rack.
Remove the pan rim, cut the tart into wedges, and serve.

storage tip

Store the dough disks in the refrigerator for up to 2 days or in the freezer for up to 1 month. If freezing the disks, wrap in plastic wrap and then place in a heavy-duty resealable plastic bag; thaw overnight in the refrigerator before using.

cook's tip

You may use a 9-inch (23-cm) round tart pan with a removable bottom instead of the tartlet pans. Roll out the dough on a floured surface, trim to a ½-inch (12-mm) overhang, and pierce with the tines of a fork. Freeze for about 15 minutes and bake until golden in a preheated 400°F (200°C) oven for about 25 minutes.

spinach & goat cheese tartlets

1 Prepare the tartlets

Preheat the oven to 400°F (200°C). Place the dough on a floured work surface and roll out to ⅛-inch (3-mm) thickness. Cut out six 5-inch (13-cm) rounds. Place each round into a 4-inch (10-cm) tartlet pan with a removable bottom. Fit the dough snugly into the corners and up the sides of the pans. Pierce the dough all over with a fork. Place on a baking sheet and freeze for 15 minutes.

2 Bake the tartlet shells

Line the dough with aluminum foil and bake until the dough edges are golden, about 15 minutes. Remove the foil and continue baking until the dough is golden brown, about 10 minutes more. Let cool on the baking sheet on a wire rack.

3 Sauté the spinach and finish the tartlets

Preheat the broiler (grill). In a large saucepan over medium heat, warm the oil. Add the garlic, and cook until golden, about 2 minutes. Using a slotted spoon, remove and discard the garlic. Add the spinach and cook until just wilted, about 2 minutes. Season with salt and pepper. Place equal amounts of spinach in each of the tartlets, top each with goat cheese, and sprinkle with the pine nuts. Broil (grill) until the cheese is golden, 2–3 minutes. Transfer the tartlets to a wire rack and let cool slightly. Remove the pan rims, slide the tarts from the pan bottoms onto individual plates, and serve at once.

Cream Cheese Dough (page 34), 1 disk, thawed

All-purpose (plain) flour, for rolling out the dough

Olive oil, 1 tablespoon

Garlic, 1 clove, smashed

Baby spinach, 1½ lb (750 g) (about 5 cups)

Salt and freshly ground pepper

Goat cheese, 4 oz (125 g), crumbled

Pine nuts, 2 tablespoons, toasted

SERVES 6

chocolate-orange turnovers

Cream Cheese Dough (page 34), 1 disk, thawed

Ricotta cheese, 1 cup (8 oz/250 g)

Powdered (icing) sugar, 3 tablespoons

Egg yolk, 1

Orange zest, from ½ orange, finely grated

Bittersweet chocolate, 1 oz (30 g), coarsely chopped

All-purpose (plain) flour, for rolling out the dough

Egg, 1 beaten, for brushing the pastry

Granulated sugar, for sprinkling

SERVES 6

1 **Prepare the filling**
In a bowl, mix together the ricotta, powdered sugar, egg yolk, orange zest, and chocolate and set aside.

2 **Prepare and bake the turnovers**
Preheat the oven to 350°F (180°C). Line a rimless baking sheet with parchment (baking) paper. On a floured work surface, roll out the dough to about ⅛-inch (3-mm) thick. Cut out six 6-inch (15-cm) rounds and place on the prepared baking sheet. Lightly brush the edges of each round with the egg mixture and spoon 2 tablespoons of the filling into the center. Fold the pastry over the filling to make half-moon shapes and press the edges with a fork to seal. Brush the tops with the remaining egg mixture and sprinkle with granulated sugar. Bake until the turnovers are golden brown, about 20 minutes. Let cool slightly on the baking sheet on a wire rack and serve warm.

cook's tip

For an almond-flavored version
of this recipe, add 3 tablespoons
finely chopped toasted almonds
and ⅛ teaspoon almond extract
(essence) in place of the orange
zest in Step 1.

cheddar-herb biscuits

CHEDDAR-HERB BISCUITS

All-purpose (plain) flour,
4 cups (20 oz/625 g), plus
more for dusting

Baking powder,
2 tablespoons

Salt, 1 teaspoon

Vegetable shortening,
½ cup (4 oz/125 g), chilled

Unsalted butter,
4 tablespoons (2 oz/60 g),
chilled and cut into cubes

Sharp Cheddar cheese,
1 cup (4 oz/125 g) shredded

Fresh chives, 2 tablespoons
chopped

Milk, 1 ½ cups (12 fl oz/
375 ml), plus more for
brushing

SERVES 4

Makes 20 biscuits total

Keep unbaked biscuits in the freezer and bake
them as needed. They can be eaten on their own,
served alongside a hearty stew, or accompanied
by bacon and eggs for a delicious breakfast.

1 Prepare the ingredients
Preheat the oven to 400°F (200°C). Line a rimless
baking sheet with parchment (baking) paper. In a large bowl,
stir together the flour, baking powder, and salt. Using a pastry
blender, cut in the shortening and butter until the mixture forms
coarse crumbs about the size of peas. Stir in the cheese and
chives. Add the milk to the dry ingredients and, using a rubber
spatula, stir just until evenly moistened.

2 Shape and bake the biscuits
Turn out the dough onto a lightly floured work surface.
and press together gently. Pat into a circle about ½ inch
(12-mm) thick. Using a floured 3-inch (7.5-cm) round biscuit
cutter, cut out rounds. Place 8 biscuits on the prepared
baking sheet and brush the tops with milk. Store the others for
future use (see Storage Tip, right). Bake until the biscuits
are golden brown, 18–20 minutes. Transfer to a wire rack, let
cool slightly, and serve.

storage tip

Unbaked biscuits freeze well.
Arrange the biscuits on a baking
sheet and place in the freezer
until solid, about 3 hours.
Transfer the biscuits to an airtight
container and freeze for up
to 2 months. Before baking, thaw
at room temperature.

cajun stew
with biscuits

1 Prepare the stew

Preheat the oven to 400°F (200°C). Line a rimless baking sheet with parchment (baking) paper. In a large saucepan over medium heat, warm the oil. Add the sausage and cook, stirring occasionally, until lightly browned, about 5 minutes. Add the onion, bell pepper, celery, and garlic and cover. Cook, stirring occasionally, until the vegetables are tender-crisp, about 5 minutes. Stir in the Cajun seasoning, tomatoes, and broth. Bring to a simmer and cook, uncovered, until the tomato juices thicken, about 15 minutes. Season with salt and pepper.

2 Bake the biscuits

Meanwhile, place the biscuits on the prepared baking sheet and brush the tops with milk. Bake until golden brown, 18–20 minutes. Split the biscuits in half crosswise and divide among shallow bowls. Ladle the stew over the biscuits, and serve.

cook's tip

To make your own Cajun spice mixture, mix together 3 tablespoons kosher salt, 1 tablespoon cayenne pepper, 1 tablespoon paprika, 2 tablespoons freshly ground black pepper, 1 teaspoon chili powder and 1 tablespoon onion powder. Store in an airtight container for up to 2 months.

Cheddar-Herb Biscuits (page 40), 8, thawed

Olive oil, 2 tablespoons

Andouille or other spicy smoked sausage, 1 lb (500 g), cut into rounds ½-inch (12-mm) thick

Yellow onion, 1, chopped

Green bell pepper (capsicum), 1, seeded and chopped

Celery, 2 stalks, chopped

Garlic, 2 cloves, minced

Cajun seasoning, 2 teaspoons, homemade (see Cook's Tip) or purchased

Canned chopped tomatoes, 1 can (28 oz/ 875 g), with juice

Chicken broth, 1 cup (8 fl oz/250 ml)

Salt and freshly ground pepper

Milk, for brushing the biscuits

SERVES 4

bacon & egg biscuits

Cheddar-Herb Biscuits (page 40), 4, thawed

Thick-sliced bacon, 4 strips, halved crosswise

Unsalted butter, 2 tablespoons

Eggs, 8

Heavy (double) cream, ¼ cup (2 fl oz/60 ml)

Salt and freshly ground pepper

Plum (Roma) tomatoes, 2, sliced

Fresh chives, 1 tablespoon finely chopped, for garnish

SERVES 4

1 **Bake the biscuits**
Preheat the oven to 400°F (200°C). Line a rimless baking sheet with parchment (baking) paper. Place the biscuits on the prepared baking sheet. Bake until golden brown, 18–20 minutes. Remove from the oven, slice crosswise, and cover to keep warm.

2 **Cook the bacon**
Meanwhile, in a large frying pan over medium heat, cook the bacon until crisp and browned, about 7 minutes. Transfer to a paper towel–lined plate to drain. Discard any excess fat and wipe the pan clean.

3 **Scramble the eggs**
Add the butter to the frying pan and melt over medium-low heat. In a large bowl, whisk together the eggs, cream, ½ teaspoon salt, and ¼ teaspoon pepper. Pour into the frying pan and cook until the edges begin to set, about 2 minutes. Using a heat-resistant rubber spatula, stir the eggs. Continue cooking, stirring occasionally, until the eggs are just set, about 2 minutes longer. Place 1 open-faced biscuit on each of 4 plates. Top each half with equal amounts of the bacon, tomatoes, and eggs, and sprinkle with chives. Serve warm.

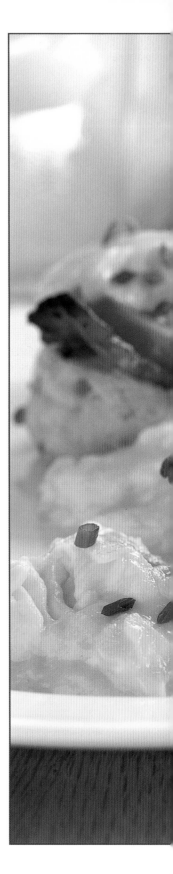

cook's tip

Poached eggs also work well
with this recipe. To make them,
bring a large pot of water to
a boil over high heat then reduce
to a simmer. Add 1 tablespoon
of white vinegar. Break the eggs
into small bowls or ramekins
and slip them into the simmering
water. Poach the eggs until the
yolks begin to set, 2–4 minutes.
Remove with a slotted spoon
and continue with Step 3.

weeknight
meals

creamy polenta with asparagus

CREAMY POLENTA

Milk, 4 cups (32 fl oz/1 l)

Salt, 1½ teaspoons

Instant polenta, 2 cups (14 oz/440 g)

Mascarpone cheese, ⅔ cup (6 oz/185 g), at room temperature

Lemon zest, from 1 lemon, finely grated

Asparagus, 1½ lb (750 g), ends trimmed

Olive oil, 1 tablespoon

Salt and freshly ground pepper

Parmesan cheese, ½ cup (2 oz/60 g) freshly grated shards

SERVES 4

Makes two 9-inch (23-cm) polenta rounds.

Cooked polenta can have two distinct textures. Served just after making, polenta makes a creamy bed for toppings such as crisp asparagus. Cooled polenta is firm enough to slice, then grill or bake.

1 Cook the asparagus
Preheat the broiler (grill). In a small bowl, mix together the mascarpone and lemon zest and set aside. Place the asparagus on a rimmed baking sheet, lightly toss with the oil, and season with salt and pepper. Broil until tender-crisp, about 6 minutes. Transfer the asparagus to a platter and cover with aluminum foil to keep warm.

2 Cook the polenta
Meanwhile, in a large saucepan over high heat, bring the milk and 3 cups (24 fl oz/750 ml) water to a boil and add 1 teaspoon salt. Whisk in the polenta. Reduce the heat to low and cook, whisking occasionally, until the polenta is thick and smooth, about 3 minutes. Leave one-third of the polenta in the pan and spread the remaining polenta into an oiled 9-inch round (23-cm) baking pans (see Storage Tip, right).

3 Finish the dish
Whisk the remaining 1 cup (8 fl oz/250 ml) milk into the polenta in the saucepan and cook until just reheated, about 30 seconds. Divide the polenta among shallow bowls and top with the asparagus. Spoon the mascarpone over the asparagus, sprinkle with the Parmesan, and serve.

storage tip

The remaining polenta can be stored in the refrigerator for up to 3 days. Spread the polenta into an oiled pan, let cool, then cover tightly with plastic wrap.

cook's tip

If you cannot find broccoli rabe,
you can use chopped kale, Swiss
chard, or other hearty greens
instead. Wash thoroughly
to remove any grit, remove the
stems and coarsely chop.

grilled polenta with sausage

1 Cook the broccoli and sausage

In a large saucepan over medium-high heat, warm 1 tablespoon of the oil. Add the sausage and sauté, stirring occasionally, until browned, about 5 minutes. Add the garlic and cook until fragrant, about 1 minute. Add the broccoli rabe and broth and bring to a boil. Reduce the heat to medium-low, cover, and simmer, stirring occasionally, until the broccoli rabe is tender-crisp, about 10 minutes. Add the red pepper flakes and season with salt.

2 Grill the polenta

Meanwhile, prepare a gas or charcoal grill for direct grilling over medium-high heat. Lightly oil the grill rack. Alternatively, preheat a grill pan over medium-high heat. Turn the polenta out onto a cutting board and cut into 8 wedges. Brush the polenta wedges with the remaining 1 tablespoon oil. Place on the grill rack or grill pan and cover. Grill, turning once, until heated through, about 5 minutes. Arrange 2 polenta wedges on each of 4 plates, spoon the sausage and broccoli alongside, and serve.

Creamy Polenta (page 48), One 9-inch (23-cm) round, at room temperature

---

Olive oil, 2 tablespoons

Italian sausages, 1 lb (500 g), casings removed and meat crumbled

Garlic, 2 cloves, minced

Broccoli rabe, 2 lb (1 kg), coarsely chopped

Chicken broth, ½ cup (4 fl oz/125 ml)

Red pepper flakes, ¼ teaspoon

Salt

SERVES 4

polenta pizza with tomato & pesto

Creamy Polenta (page 48), One 9-inch (23-cm) round, at room temperature

Pesto, ¼ cup (2 fl oz/60 ml), purchased

Tomato, 1 large, sliced

Fresh mozzarella, 8 oz (250 g), sliced

Olive oil, for brushing the polenta

SERVES 4–6

1 Prepare the pizza
Preheat the oven to 400°F (200°C). Turn the polenta out onto a rimmed baking sheet lined with parchment (baking) paper. Spread the top of the polenta with the pesto, leaving a ½-inch (12-mm) wide border. Top with the tomato slices, and divide the cheese evenly over the top. Brush the exposed polenta with oil.

2 Bake the pizza
Bake until the cheese is melted and the polenta is golden, 20–25 minutes. Let cool briefly on the baking sheet on a wire rack. Transfer to a cutting board, cut into wedges, and serve.

cook's tip

Ripe tomatoes should be firm and fully colored. They are at their peak during the warm days of summer. When baking ripe tomatoes, it is a good idea to salt them to draw out any excess moisture. Pat dry before using.

salt & pepper chicken

CHICKEN BREASTS

Bone-in, skin-on chicken breast halves, 6, about 4 lb (2 kg) total weight

Salt and freshly ground pepper

Chicken broth, 1 cup (8 fl oz/250 ml)

Fresh thyme, sage, or tarragon, 1 teaspoon chopped

Unsalted butter, 2 tablespoons, chilled and cut into cubes

SERVES 4

Makes about 8 cups (3 lb/1.5 kg) cooked chicken total

It takes little effort to roast extra chicken breasts in order to have leftover chicken for another meal. The breasts are simply seasoned with pepper, salt, and herbs to make them versatile.

1 Roast the chicken
Preheat the oven to 400°F (200°C). Season the chicken generously with salt and pepper on top of and under the skin. Place the chicken skin side up in a large roasting pan. Roast until the chicken is golden brown and an instant-read thermometer inserted into the center of each breast reads 170°F (77°C), about 45 minutes. Transfer 4 chicken breasts to a serving platter, and reserve the remaining 2 for another use (see Storage Tip, right).

2 Deglaze the pan
Place the pan on the stove top over high heat. When the pan sizzles, add the broth and thyme and stir to scrape up the browned pits from the pan bottom. Boil until the broth is reduced by half, about 3 minutes. Remove from the heat.

3 Make the sauce
Whisk the butter, a couple of pieces at a time, into the reduced liquid. Season with salt and pepper. Serve the chicken, passing the sauce at the table.

storage tip

To store the chicken for use in the following recipes, let it cool, then remove the meat, discarding the skin and bones. Shred the meat and store in an airtight container or resealable plastic bag in the refrigerator for up to 3 days. It is best not to freeze poultry or meat once it has been cooked.

chicken tostada salad

1 Prepare the salsa

In a bowl, whisk together the lime zest and juice, and garlic with ½ teaspoon salt and ⅛ teaspoon pepper. Slowly whisk in the oil. Transfer 3 tablespoons of the vinaigrette to a large bowl and add the beans, corn, tomatoes, and chiles; mix gently. Reserve the remaining vinaigrette. Let the salsa stand for at least 10 minutes until the flavors have blended.

2 Assemble the salads

Add the lettuce to the reserved vinaigrette and toss to coat. Divide the tostadas and lettuce among 4 plates. Spoon the salsa over the lettuce, top with the chicken, and serve.

cook's tip

Deep-fried tostadas are available in most well-stocked supermarkets. If you cannot find them, divide 4 cups of good-quality corn tortilla chips among bowls, top with the chicken salad, and serve.

Salt & Pepper Chicken (page 54), 2 cups (12 oz/ 375 g), shredded

Lime zest and juice, from 2 limes

Garlic, 1 clove, minced

Salt and freshly ground pepper

Olive oil, ⅔ cup (5 fl oz/ 160 ml)

Black beans, 1 can (4½ oz/ 455 g), drained and rinsed

Fresh corn kernels, from 2 ears of corn (about 2 cups/ 12 oz/ 375 g)

Plum (Roma) tomatoes, 2, seeded and diced

Canned green chiles, 4, diced

Romaine (cos) lettuce, 1 small head, cut into bite-sized pieces

Corn tostadas, 4

SERVES 4

shanghai noodles
with chicken

Salt & Pepper Chicken (page 54), 2 cups (12 oz/ 375 g) shredded

Fresh Chinese egg noodles, 1 lb (500 g)

Asian dark sesame oil, 1 tablespoon

Peanut or canola oil, 2 tablespoons

Garlic, 1 clove, minced

Fresh ginger, 1 tablespoon finely grated

Red pepper flakes, ¼ teaspoon

Bok choy, 3 cups (10 oz/ 280 g), cut into wide strips

Carrot, 1, cut into thin matchsticks

Green (spring) onions, 2, white and pale green parts only, cut into 1-inch (2.5-cm) slices

Chicken broth, ½ cup (4 fl oz/125 ml)

Oyster sauce, 3 tablespoons

SERVES 4

1 Boil the noodles
Bring a large pot of water to a boil over high heat. Separate the strands of noodles, drop them into the boiling water, and boil for 2 minutes. Drain, rinse under cold running water, and drain again. Toss the noodles with the sesame oil and set aside.

2 Stir-fry the vegetables
In a wok or large frying pan over high heat, warm the peanut oil. Add the garlic and ginger and stir until fragrant, about 10 seconds. Stir in the red pepper flakes, bok choy, carrot, and the white part of the green onions. Stir-fry the vegetables until the bok choy wilts, about 2 minutes. Meanwhile, in a small bowl, combine the broth and oyster sauce and set aside.

3 Stir-fry the noodles
Add the noodles, chicken, and broth mixture to the wok and toss to combine. Cook, stirring often, until the noodles and chicken are heated through, about 2 minutes. Stir in the tops of the green onions and serve.

cook's tip

It is always best to start with good quality fresh pasta. Fresh Chinese egg noodles can be found in well-stocked markets and Asian grocery stores. If you cannot find fresh noodles, you can substitute dried spaghetti. Be sure to follow the directions on the package as the cooking time will differ.

baked ham with green beans

BAKED HAM

Smoked ham on the bone, 7½ lb (3.75 kg), fat trimmed and scored

Orange juice, 1 cup (8 fl oz/250 ml)

Green beans, 2 lb (1 kg), trimmed

Shallots, 2, minced

Salt and freshly ground pepper

SERVES 6–8

Makes about 8 cups (5 lb/2.5 kg) sliced or cubed ham total

A baked ham is perfect for leftovers. Bake the ham tonight and you'll have enough to make rich croque monsieurs, hearty black bean soup, or delicious pasta with peas and ham in the days that follow.

1 Bake the ham
Preheat the oven to 325°F (165°C). Place the ham in a large roasting pan and pour the orange juice into the pan bottom. Cover the pan tightly with aluminum foil and bake for 1 hour. Remove the foil and continue to roast until completely heated through, about 1 hour longer. Baste the ham occasionally during the last hour of cooking. Bake until an instant-read thermometer inserted into the thickest part of the ham, away from the bone, reads 160°F (71°C). Transfer to a carving board and let rest for 20 minutes.

2 Prepare the green beans
While the ham is resting, pour off all but 2 tablespoons of the fat from the roasting pan. Add the green beans and shallots, season with salt and pepper, and toss to combine. Return the pan to the oven and roast, stirring occasionally, until the green beans are tender-crisp, about 15 minutes.

3 Carve the ham
Slice the ham and arrange on individual plates with the green beans. Let the remaining ham cool, then store for later use (see Storage Tip, right).

storage tip

Leftover ham can be cooled, wrapped in plastic wrap, and stored in the refrigerator for up to 1 week. Freezing compromises the flavor and texture of the ham, so plan to use refrigerated leftovers the same week you bake the ham.

cook's tip

For another meal, make
sandwiches with mango chutney
and extra-sharp Cheddar cheese
instead of the Gruyère and Dijon
mustard. This version is especially
good on whole-grain bread.

baked
croque monsieurs

1 Make the sauce

Preheat the oven to 400°F (200°C). In a saucepan over low heat, melt the butter. Add the flour and whisk until smooth. Let bubble, whisking constantly and without browning, for 1 minute. Slowly whisk in the hot milk, raise the heat to medium, and bring to a simmer. Simmer, whisking often, until thickened, about 5 minutes. Remove from the heat, stir in ½ cup (4 oz/125 g) of the Gruyère, and season with salt and pepper. Remove from the heat and let stand, stirring often, until cooled.

2 Toast the bread

Arrange the bread slices on a large baking sheet lined with parchment (baking) paper. Toast the bread, turning once, until golden, about 10 minutes total. Remove from the oven and set aside.

3 Bake the sandwiches

Raise the oven temperature to broil (grill). Spread 4 bread slices with the mustard, add 1 slice of ham, 1 tablespoon of the sauce, and top with the remaining bread slices. Spread the remaining sauce over the tops of the sandwiches, being sure to cover the edges, and sprinkle with the remaining ¼ cup (1 oz/30 g) of Gruyère. Broil (grill) until the cheese is melted and golden brown, about 2 minutes. Transfer to individual plates and serve.

Baked Ham (page 60),
4 slices

Unsalted butter,
2 tablespoons

All-purpose (plain) flour,
2 tablespoons

Milk, 1 cup (8 fl oz/250 ml),
heated

Gruyère cheese, ¾ cup
(3 oz/90 g) shredded

**Salt and freshly ground
pepper**

**Country-style white
sandwich bread,** 8 slices

Dijon mustard,
4 tablespoons

SERVES 4

black bean soup
with ham

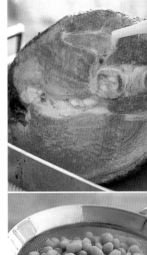

Baked Ham (page 60), 1 cup (6 oz/185 g), diced

Olive oil, 2 tablespoons

Yellow onion, 1, finely chopped

Carrots, 2, finely chopped

Celery, 1 stalk, finely chopped

Garlic, 2 cloves, minced

Black beans, 2 cans, (14½ oz/455 g each), drained and rinsed

Chicken broth, 6 cups (48 fl oz/1.5 l)

Dry sherry, ½ cup (4 fl oz/ 125 ml)

Salt and freshly ground pepper

Sour cream, ¼ cup (2 oz/ 60 g), for garnish

SERVES 8

1 Prepare the soup

In a large saucepan over medium heat, warm the oil. Add the onion, carrot, and celery. Cook, stirring occasionally, until the vegetables begin to soften, about 5 minutes. Add the garlic and cook until fragrant, about 1 minute longer. Add the black beans, chicken broth, and sherry. Cover and bring to a boil over high heat. Reduce the heat to medium-low and simmer, partially covered and stirring often, until the flavors have blended, about 15 minutes.

2 Finish the soup

In a blender or food processor purée 2 cups (16 fl oz/ 500 ml) of the soup, then return to the pan. Add the ham and simmer over medium heat until the ham is heated through, about 5 minutes. Season with salt and pepper. Ladle the soup into bowls, garnish with the sour cream, and serve.

cook's tip

This soup can easily be turned into a white bean soup. Substitute cannellini or Great Northern beans for the black beans, drain and rinse, and omit the sherry and sour cream.

cook's tip

If you prefer, substitute 1 cup
(6 oz/185 g) chopped cooked
pancetta or thick-cut bacon
for the ham. Both will add
a pleasant, smoky note to the
creamy sauce.

pappardelle with ham & peas

1 Make the sauce
Bring a large pot of water to a boil. In a large frying pan over medium heat, melt the butter. Add the ham and cook, stirring occasionally, until lightly browned, about 5 minutes. Add the cream and bring to a gentle boil. Stir in the peas and season to taste with salt and pepper. Keep warm over low heat.

2 Cook the pasta
Meanwhile, add 2 tablespoons salt and the pasta to the boiling water. Cook, stirring occasionally to prevent sticking, until the pasta is al dente, according to the package directions. Drain, reserving about ½ cup (4 fl oz/125 ml) of the cooking water. Add the pasta to the sauce along with ½ cup (2 oz/60 g) of the Parmesan. Toss to combine. Warm briefly over low heat to blend the flavors. Add as much of the cooking water as needed to loosen the sauce. Serve, passing the remaining Parmesan at the table.

Baked Ham (page 60), 1 cup (6 oz/185 g) diced

Unsalted butter, 2 tablespoons

Heavy (double) cream, 1 cup (8 fl oz/250 ml)

Frozen peas, 1½ cups (8 oz/ 250 g), thawed

Salt and freshly ground pepper

Pappardelle or wide egg noodles, 1 lb (500 g)

Parmesan cheese, 1 cup (4 oz/125 g) freshly grated

SERVES 4

beef salad with mango

BEEF ROAST

Top loin beef roast, 6 lb (3 kg), trimmed of excess fat

Salt and freshly ground black pepper

Asian fish sauce or soy sauce, 1 tablespoon

Lime juice, from 1 lime

Canola oil, ⅓ cup (3 fl oz/80 ml)

Asian sesame oil, 1 tablespoon

Mango, 2 large, peeled, pitted, and sliced

Red bell pepper (capsicum), 1, seeded and thinly sliced

Shallot, 1 large, thinly sliced

Mixed greens, 4 cups (4 oz/125 g)

Fresh mint, 2 tablespoons slivered

SERVES 4

Makes about 10 cups (4 lb/2 kg) sliced or shredded beef total

Prepare a large beef roast and you'll have enough extra beef for at least two more meals. The roast has a smokiness that enhances the flavor of a sweet and spicy salad, a beef hash and a spicy Thai curry.

1 **Roast the beef**
Preheat the oven to 350°F (180°C). Season the beef generously with salt and pepper and place in a shallow roasting pan just large enough to hold it comfortably. Roast, turning occasionally, until an instant-read thermometer inserted into the center of the beef reads 130°F (54°C) for medium-rare, about 1¼ hours, or until the desired level of doneness. Transfer to a carving board and let rest for 10–15 minutes before carving.

2 **Assemble the salad**
Thinly slice 4 portions of the beef, reserving the remaining beef for other meals (see Storage Tip, right). Cut each slice into strips. In a large bowl, whisk together the fish sauce, lime zest and juice. Whisk in the canola and sesame oils. Add the beef, mango, bell pepper, and shallot and toss evenly with the vinaigrette. Divide the greens among individual plates and top with the beef-mango mixture. Sprinkle with the mint and serve.

storage tip

To store the remaining beef, let the roast cool to room temperature, wrap tightly in aluminum foil or plastic wrap, and refrigerate for up to 3 days. For the most succulent and tender results, do not slice the chilled beef until ready to serve. To slice, use a chef's or other large, sharp knife, and thinly slice across the grain.

cook's tip

For a spicier dish, add additional seeded and minced chile peppers. Use kitchen gloves to protect your hands while mincing and seeding the chiles, as they contain oils that may irritate your skin.

steak hash & eggs

1 Sauté the vegetables

Preheat the oven to 200°F (95°C). In a large frying pan over medium heat, melt the butter. Add the potato and ¼ cup (2 fl oz/60 ml) water. Cover and cook until the potato is almost tender and the water is absorbed, about 15 minutes. Add the onion, bell pepper, chile, and garlic. Cook, stirring often, until the vegetables soften, about 6 minutes. Add the beef and cook until heated through, about 3 minutes. Season with salt and pepper and divide the hash among individual plates.

2 Cook the eggs

In a large frying pan over medium heat, warm the oil. Working with 1 egg at a time, break the eggs into the pan, cover and reduce the heat to low. Cook until the eggs reach the desired level of doneness, about 3 minutes. Place 1 egg on top of each serving of hash and serve.

Beef Roast (page 68),
2 cups (12 oz/375 g) diced

Unsalted butter,
3 tablespoons

Russet potato, 1 large
peeled and cut into ½-inch
(12-mm) chunks

Yellow onion, 1, chopped

**Red bell pepper
(capsicum),** 1 small, seeded
and chopped

Jalapeño chile, 1, seeded
and finely chopped

Garlic, 1 clove, minced

**Salt and freshly ground
pepper**

Olive oil, 2 tablespoons

Eggs, 4

SERVES 4

thai
beef curry

Beef Roast (page 68),
2 cups (12 oz/375 g) cubed

Canola oil, 2 tablespoons

Yellow onion, 1 large, halved and thinly sliced

Fresh ginger, 1 tablespoon, finely grated

Thai red curry paste, 1 tablespoon

Red-skinned potatoes, 3 medium, cut into ½-inch (12-mm) dice

Unsweetened coconut milk, 1 can (13½ fl oz/ 420 ml)

Salt and freshly ground pepper

Baby spinach, 4 cups packed (4 oz/125 g)

Steamed rice, for serving

SERVES 4

1 **Prepare the vegetables**
In a large saucepan over medium heat, warm the oil. Add the onion and cook, stirring, until golden, about 5 minutes. Add the ginger and cook until fragrant, about 1 minute. Stir in the curry paste. Add the potatoes, coconut milk, and 1 cup (8 fl oz/250 ml) water and bring to a gentle boil. Reduce the heat to low and simmer, covered, until the potatoes are tender, about 20 minutes. Season with salt and pepper.

2 **Finish the curry**
Add the beef and spinach to the saucepan and simmer until the spinach is wilted and the beef is heated through, about 2 minutes. Divide the rice among bowls, top with the curry, and serve.

cook's tip

Curry paste comes in a variety
of heat levels, each with a distinct
flavor. For this recipe, red curry
paste is used, but you can easily
substitute green curry. Green
curry paste, made from a number
of different ingredients including
Thai basil and green chiles,
is milder than red curry, so you
may want to add a bit more
of it when using.

freeze it

three-cheese manicotti

Manicotti, 14 (1 lb/500 g)

Roasted tomato sauce, 3 cups (24 fl oz/750 ml), homemade (page 16) or purchased

Ricotta cheese, 2½ cups (1¼ lb/625 g)

Fresh mozzarella cheese, 8 oz (250 g), cut into small pieces

Parmesan cheese, ¾ cup (3 oz/90 g) freshly grated

Fresh basil, ¼ cup (⅓ oz/ 10 g) chopped

Eggs, 2, beaten

Salt and freshly ground pepper

Freshly grated nutmeg, ⅛ teaspoon

SERVES 6

1 Cook the manicotti
Lightly oil a 9-by-13-inch (23-by-33-cm) freezer-to-oven baking dish. Bring a large pot of water to a boil over high heat. Add 2 tablespoons salt and the manicotti. Cook, stirring occasionally to prevent sticking, until the pasta is not quite al dente, about 2 minutes less than the package directions. Drain, rinse under cold running water, and drain again.

2 Fill the manicotti
Preheat the oven to 350°F (180°C). Spread a thin layer of the tomato sauce in the baking dish. In a large bowl, mix together the ricotta and mozzarella cheeses, ½ cup (2 oz/60 g) of the Parmesan, the basil, eggs, ½ teaspoon salt, ¼ teaspoon pepper, and the nutmeg. Place the cheese mixture in a pastry bag or a large ziploc bag with one bottom corner snipped off, and fill the manicotti. Place the filled manicotti in the prepared dish and top with the remaining tomato sauce and Parmesan cheese. If freezing, cover the dish tightly with aluminum foil and set aside (see Freezing Tip, right).

3 Bake the manicotti
Cover the dish with aluminum foil. Bake until the sauce is bubbling and the cheese is golden, about 35 minutes. Let stand 10 minutes before serving.

freezing tip

The manicotti can be frozen for up to 1 month. To freeze, cover the dish tightly with aluminum foil. Bake, frozen and covered, at 350°F (180°C), for 1 hour.

freezing tip

To freeze, transfer the macaroni
and cheese to a buttered
9-by-13-inch (23-by-33-cm)
freezer-to-oven baking dish.
Cover tightly with aluminum
foil. Freeze for up to 2 months.
Bake, frozen and covered,
at 350°F (180°C), for 1 hour.
Uncover, top with the bread
cubes, and bake until the
topping is golden, about
20 minutes longer.

macaroni & cheese

1 **Prepare the sauce**
Preheat the oven to 350°F (180°C). Butter four 1-cup (8 fl oz/250 ml) individual ramekins or a 3-qt (3-l) freezer-to-oven baking dish. Bring a large pot of water to a boil over high heat. In a large saucepan over low heat, melt 6 tablespoons (3 oz/90 g) of the butter. Add the flour, a little at a time, whisking to incorporate. Raise the heat to medium and very gradually whisk in the heated milk. Cook, stirring frequently, until the mixture is thick and creamy, about 10 minutes. Remove from the heat. Add the Cheddar, fontina, and mustard and whisk until the cheese is melted. Set aside.

2 **Cook the macaroni**
Meanwhile, add 2 tablespoons salt and the macaroni to the boiling water. Cook, stirring occasionally to prevent sticking, until the pasta is not quite al dente, about 2 minutes less than the package directions. Drain well. Add the pasta to the cheese sauce and stir well. Season to taste with salt and pepper. Transfer to the ramekins or baking dish. If freezing, set aside and let cool (see Freezing Tip, left).

3 **Bake the macaroni and cheese**
In a frying pan, melt the remaining 2 tablespoons butter in a medium frying pan. Remove from the heat, add the bread crumbs and stir until coated. Sprinkle over the macaroni and cheese. Bake until the sauce is bubbling, about 30 minutes. Let stand 5 minutes, then serve.

Unsalted butter,
8 tablespoons (4 oz/125 g), plus more for brushing

All-purpose (plain) flour,
½ cup (2½ oz/75 g)

Milk, 1 qt (32 fl oz/1 l), heated

Sharp Cheddar cheese,
4 cups (1 lb/500 g) shredded

Fontina cheese, 2 oz (60 g), shredded

Dry mustard, 2 teaspoons

Salt and freshly ground pepper

Macaroni, shells, or penne,
1 lb (500 g)

Fresh coarse bread crumbs, from 4 slices country-style white bread

SERVES 4

classic
crab cakes

Eggs, 2

Mayonnaise, ½ cup
(4 fl oz/125 ml)

Dijon mustard,
2 tablespoons

Worcestershire sauce,
2 tablespoons

Hot sauce, ½ teaspoon

Fresh lump crabmeat,
2 lb (1 kg), picked over for
shell fragments and squeezed
to remove excess water

Dried bread crumbs,
½ cup (1 oz/30 g)

Fresh chives, 4 tablespoons

Canola oil, ⅔ cup
(5 fl oz/160 ml)

Mixed greens, 4 cups
(4 oz/125 g)

Lemon wedges, for serving

SERVES 6

1 Prepare the crab cakes
In a large bowl, beat the eggs lightly. Add the
mayonnaise, mustard, Worcestershire sauce, hot sauce,
crabmeat, bread crumbs, and chives. Stir with a fork
until well mixed. Gently form the mixture into small patties
about 1½ inches (4 cm) in diameter. You should have
18–20 patties. Transfer to a baking sheet and refrigerate
for 15–30 minutes to allow the cakes to firm slightly.
If freezing, place in the freezer (see Freezing Tip, right).

2 Cook the crab cakes
In a large frying pan over medium heat, warm the oil.
Working in batches if necessary, add the crab cakes and cook,
without moving them, until golden brown on the first sides,
about 4 minutes. Turn and cook until golden brown on the
second sides, 3–4 minutes longer. Divide the greens among
individual plates, top with 2–3 crab cakes, and serve with the
lemon wedges alongside.

freezing tip

To freeze, place the uncooked
crab cakes on a baking sheet
in the freezer just until firm,
about 2 hours. Wrap each cake
in plastic wrap and place in
a plastic freezer bag. Freeze for
up to 1 month. Defrost the
crab cakes in the refrigerator
overnight before cooking.

freezing tip

To freeze, place the uncooked salmon cakes on a baking sheet in the freezer just until firm, about 2 hours. Wrap each cake

in plastic wrap and place in a plastic freezer bag. Freeze for up to 1 month. Defrost in the refrigerator overnight before cooking.

asian
salmon cakes

1 Prepare the salmon

Preheat the oven to 400°F (200°C). Lightly oil a rimmed baking sheet. Place the salmon on the baking sheet and season lightly with salt and pepper. Bake until the fish is barely opaque when flaked in the thickest part, about 20 minutes. Remove from the oven and let cool completely. Using a fork, break the salmon into large flakes.

2 Prepare the salmon cakes

Line a rimmed baking sheet with parchment (baking) paper. In a large bowl, whisk together the oyster sauce, egg yolks, green onions, ginger, and garlic. Add the flaked salmon and 1 cup (2½ oz/75 g) of the panko and mix with a fork until combined. Gently form the mixture into small patties, about 1½ inches (4 cm) in diameter. Coat the cakes on both sides with the remaining panko and place on the baking sheet. Refrigerate for 15–30 minutes to allow the cakes to firm slightly. If freezing, place in the freezer (see Freezing Tip, left).

3 Make the sauce and cook the cakes

Meanwhile, make the dipping sauce. In a small bowl, mix together the soy sauce and lime juice and pour into 8 ramekins or small bowls. In a large frying pan over medium-high heat, warm the oil. Add the salmon cakes and cook until golden brown on the first sides, about 3 minutes. Turn and cook until golden brown on the second sides, about 3 minutes longer. Divide the salmon cakes among individual plates and serve with the soy-lime dipping sauce.

Salmon fillets, 2, about 3 lb (1.5 kg) total weight, skin removed

Salt and freshly ground pepper

Oyster sauce, 6 tablespoons (3 fl oz/90 ml)

Egg yolks, 2

Green (spring) onions, white and pale green parts, 4, finely chopped

Fresh ginger, 2 tablespoons, finely grated

Garlic, 2 cloves, minced

***Panko* or fine dried bread crumbs,** 2 cups (5 oz/150 g)

Soy sauce, 1 cup (8 fl oz/ 250 ml)

Juice from 4 limes

Canola oil, ¼ cup (2 fl oz/60 ml)

SERVES 8

chicken chili
with beans

Olive oil, 3 tablespoons

Boneless, skinless chicken thighs, 2½ lb (1.25 kg), cut into 1-inch (2.5 cm) chunks

Yellow onion, 1 large, chopped

Red bell pepper (capsicum), 1 large, seeded and chopped

Garlic, 2 cloves, minced

Jalapeño chile, 1, seeded and minced

Chili powder, 2 tablespoons

Diced tomatoes, 1 can (28 oz/875 g), with juice

Pinto beans, 2 cans (14½ oz/ 455 g each), drained and rinsed

Salt and freshly ground pepper

Fresh cilantro (coriander), 3 tablespoons chopped

SERVES 6–8

1 **Cook the chicken**
In a large saucepan over medium-high heat, warm the oil. Add the chicken and cook, stirring once or twice, until golden, 5–7 minutes total. Using a slotted spoon, transfer the chicken to a plate.

2 **Prepare the vegetables**
Add the onion, bell pepper, garlic, and chile to the pan and sauté, stirring occasionally, until softened, about 5 minutes. Stir in the chili powder and return the chicken and any juices from the plate to the pan. Add the tomatoes and their juices and 1 cup (8 fl oz/250 ml) water and bring to a simmer. Cover, reduce the heat to medium-low, and simmer, stirring once or twice, until the chicken is opaque throughout and the chili has thickened, about 15 minutes.

3 **Finish the chili**
Stir in the beans and cook until they are heated through, about 5 minutes. Season with salt and pepper. Ladle the chili into individual bowls, garnish with the cilantro, and serve.

freezing tip

To freeze, let the chili cool to room temperature. Store in airtight containers in the freezer for up to 3 months. Thaw overnight in the refrigerator and reheat over low heat, adding water, if needed, to loosen the chili. Garnish with the cilantro just before serving.

freezing tip

To freeze, fill a large bowl or your sink with ice water. Pour the soup into a smaller bowl and nest in the ice. Stir the soup occasionally to hasten cooling. Once cooled, transfer the chowder to 1-qt (1-l) airtight containers, leaving ½ inch (12 mm) of headroom to allow for expansion. Freeze for up to 2 months. Thaw overnight in the refrigerator and reheat over medium-low heat.

chicken & corn chowder

1 Cook the leeks and chicken

In a large saucepan over medium heat, warm the oil. Add the leeks and cover. Cook, stirring occasionally, until softened, about 3 minutes. Add the chicken and cover. Cook, stirring occasionally, just until the chicken is golden on all sides, about 5 minutes.

2 Prepare the chowder

Add the broth, potatoes, thyme, ½ teaspoon salt, and ½ teaspoon pepper. Cover and bring to a boil over high heat. Reduce the heat to medium and simmer, partially covered, until the potatoes are tender, about 30 minutes.

3 Finish the chowder

In a bowl, mix together the butter and flour to form a paste. Whisk 1 cup (8 fl oz/250 ml) of the broth into the mixture and add to the saucepan along with the corn. Return to a simmer and cook, stirring frequently, until thickened, about 5 minutes. Stir in the cream and season with salt and pepper. Ladle the chowder into bowls and serve. If freezing, set aside to cool (see Freezing Tip, left).

Canola oil, 2 tablespoons

Leeks, 3, white and pale green parts only, chopped

Boneless, skinless chicken thighs, 2½ lb (1.25 kg), cut into 1-inch (2.5-cm) pieces

Chicken broth, 2 qt (2 l)

Red-skinned potatoes, 3, cut into 1-inch (2.5-cm) peeled and diced

Fresh thyme, 1 teaspoon finely chopped

Salt and freshly ground pepper

Unsalted butter, 4 tablespoons, (2 oz/60 g), at room temperature

All-purpose (plain) flour, ¼ cup (1½ oz/45 g)

Corn kernels, 1½ cups (7 oz/220 g)

Heavy (double) cream, ½ cup (4 fl oz/125 ml)

SERVES 8

bacon, gruyére & spinach quiche

Cream Cheese Dough (page 34), 1 disk, thawed, or purchased pie crust

Thick-sliced bacon, 6 strips, chopped

Shallot, 1, minced

Baby spinach, 6 cups (6 oz/ 185 g)

Eggs, 3 large

Milk, 1½ cups (12 fl oz/ 375 ml)

Salt and freshly ground pepper

Nutmeg, ⅛ teaspoon freshly grated

Gruyère cheese, ½ cup (2 oz/60 g) shredded

SERVES 6

1 Prepare the pastry shell
Position a rack in the middle of the oven and preheat to 400°F (200°C). On a floured work surface, roll out the dough into a 12-inch (30-cm) round. Fit into a 9-inch (23-cm) round tart pan and trim the dough to a ½-inch (12-mm) overhang. Fold the overhang back over itself and pinch to create a sturdy edge. Pierce the dough all over with a fork. Freeze for 15 minutes. Bake until the edges are lightly golden, about 15 minutes. Let cool briefly on a wire rack. Reduce the oven temperature to 375°F (190°C) .

2 Make the filling
In a frying pan over medium heat, cook the bacon until crisp, about 8 minutes. Transfer to a paper towel–lined plate. Pour off all but 1 tablespoon of the fat from the pan, add the shallot, and cook just until softened, about 1 minute. Stir in the spinach and cook until wilted, about 3 minutes. In a bowl, whisk together the eggs, milk, ¼ teaspoon salt, ¼ teaspoon pepper, and the nutmeg. Add the spinach mixture to the bowl and mix to combine.

3 Bake the quiche
Sprinkle the bacon and Gruyère in the partially baked pastry shell. Pour in the spinach mixture. Bake until the filling is set and the crust is golden, 30–35 minutes. Let cool briefly on a wire rack. Cut into wedges and serve warm. If freezing, set aside to cool (see Freezing Tip, right).

freezing tip

To freeze, let the baked quiche cool completely. Wrap in aluminum foil and freeze for up to 2 months. To reheat, place the unwrapped quiche on a baking sheet and bake in a preheated 325°F (165°C) oven until heated through, about 40 minutes.

freezing tip

To freeze, let the soup cool
completely. Transfer the soup
to 1-qt (1-l) airtight containers,
leaving ½ inch (12 mm) at the
top to allow for expansion. Freeze
the soup for up to 2 months.
Thaw overnight in the refrigerator,
and reheat over medium heat.

hearty beef & vegetable soup

1 Sauté the beef

In a large saucepan over medium-high heat, warm 1 tablespoon of the oil. In batches, add the beef and cook, stirring occasionally, until browned, about 4 minutes. Transfer to a plate and set aside.

2 Cook the vegetables

Add the remaining 1 tablespoon oil to the saucepan and reduce the heat to medium. Add the onion, carrots, and celery and cover. Cook, stirring occasionally, until the onion is softened, about 5 minutes. Return the beef and any juices from the plate to the pan.

3 Simmer the soup

Add 1½ qt (1.5 l) water to the pan and bring to a boil over high heat. Reduce the heat to medium-low and simmer, partially covered, for 1 hour. Add the potatoes, the tomatoes and their juice, and the green beans, and stir well. Simmer until the beef and the potatoes are tender, about 20 minutes. Stir in the parsley and season to taste with salt and pepper. Ladle the soup into individual bowls, and serve. If freezing, set aside to cool (see Freezing Tip, left).

Olive oil, 2 tablespoons

Boneless beef chuck, 1 lb (500 g), cut into chunks

Yellow onion, 1 large, chopped

Carrots, 2, chopped

Celery, 2 stalks, chopped

Red-skinned potatoes, 2, scrubbed but unpeeled, cut into chunks

Crushed plum (Roma) tomatoes, 1 can (28 oz/ 875 g), with juice

Green beans, ½ lb (250 g), trimmed

Fresh flat-leaf (Italian) parsley, 2 tablespoons chopped

Salt and freshly ground pepper

SERVES 6–8

penne with winter squash & pancetta

Olive oil, 1 tablespoon

Pancetta or thick-sliced bacon, 4 oz (125 g), coarsely chopped

Butternut or other winter squash, 1 lb (500 g), peeled, seeded, and cut into 1-inch (2.5-cm) pieces

Kale, 12 oz (375 g), stems removed and leaves chopped

Chicken broth, 2 cups (16 fl oz/500 ml)

Heavy (double) cream, ½ cup (4 fl oz/125 ml)

Fresh sage, 2 teaspoons chopped

Salt and freshly ground pepper

Penne or other medium-sized pasta, 1 lb (500 g)

SERVES 4

1 Make the sauce
Bring a large pot of water to a boil over high heat. In a large frying pan over medium heat, warm the oil. Add the pancetta and cook, stirring occasionally, until browned, about 5 minutes. Using a slotted spoon, transfer the pancetta to a paper towel–lined plate. Pour off all but 2 tablespoons of fat from the pan. Add the squash and kale and sauté until the kale begins to wilt, about 1 minute. Add the broth, cover, and cook until the squash is just tender, about 15 minutes. Uncover and bring to a boil over high heat. Let cook until the broth is reduced by half, about 5 minutes longer. Reduce the heat to low and stir in the cream and sage. Season with salt and pepper. To freeze the sauce, set aside to cool (see Freezing Tip, right).

2 Cook the pasta
Meanwhile, add 2 tablespoons salt and the pasta to the boiling water. Cook, stirring occasionally, until al dente, according to the package directions. Drain, reserving about ½ cup (4 fl oz/125 ml) of the cooking water.

3 Finish the pasta
Add the pasta to the sauce along with the reserved pancetta. Toss to combine over low heat. Add as much of the cooking water as needed to loosen the sauce and serve.

freezing tip
To freeze, remove the sauce from the heat and let cool completely. Transfer to a 1-qt (1-l) airtight container and

freeze for up to 2 months. Thaw in the refrigerator. When reheating the sauce, stir in an additional 2 tablespoons cream.

the smarter cook

The secret to getting dinner on the table during a hectic workweek isn't spending more time in the kitchen, it's cooking smarter. And you can do just that with inspired recipes, a weekly menu, and a shopping list for the week. This book will teach you how to make double batches of sauces or meats and then use the leftovers in multiple delicious and creative meals throughout the week or store whole meals in the freezer for a homemade supper anytime.

By keeping your pantry well-stocked you are on your way to having what you need to make last-minute meals. Using the seasons for inspiration and, as much as possible, shopping for local produce at the height of its flavor, will help you create more memorable fare with a minimum of fuss.

get started

Three simple strategies will make your kitchen run like clockwork. First, draw up a weekly meal plan so you can easily see where you can create make-ahead components and streamline your shopping. Next, keep your pantry, refrigerator, and freezer well stocked with key ingredients. Finally, use seasonal produce to add variety and superior flavor to your meals.

■ **Plan your menus for the week.** Use free time over the weekend to devise a menu plan for the entire week ahead. Include dishes that make large batches to ensure leftovers, and recipes that use premade components to save time. Vary the types of dishes you select, serving a stir-fry for one meal and a grilled dish on another night.

■ **Make menus to fit your schedule.** As you map out your commitments for the week ahead, be realistic about the time you have to make dinner. Also, if you choose a main course that you've made ahead and frozen, don't forget to allow time to thaw it.

■ **Cook large batches.** Select a main course from Weeknight Meals to serve as one night's dinner, and you'll have leftovers to use for subsequent meals. Some of these recipes may take some time to cook, but when you spread that time out over future meals, you'll discover that you've actually saved time. Or, make a double recipe from Freeze It and have dinner tonight plus a main course for another meal.

■ **Let the seasons be your guide.** Vegetables and fruits at the peak of their season have more flavor, cost less, and add variety to your cooking. Preserve this flavor by using produce in sauces and pestos that can be served later. To keep the kitchen cool during hot weather, grill meals outside. And when the temperature drops, prepare warming soups and stews to take off the chill.

■ **Get everyone involved.** When making your weekly menu plan, ask family members what they would like to eat. And when dinner time comes around, let everyone pitch in—washing salad greens, chopping vegetables, setting the table—to get the meal on the table.

THINK SEASONALLY

While the recipes in this book can be made throughout the year, they will be at their best when seasonal produce is used. Here are some ideas to inspire you.

spring Take advantage of tender, young greens; first-of-the-season herbs like mint, tarragon, and chives; new potatoes; and sugar snap peas. Light mains, such as fish cakes and salads, will prove to be the most appetizing.

summer Fire up the grill to cook with the season's abundant bell peppers (capsicums), eggplants (aubergines), corn, and zucchini (courgettes).

autumn This is the time to allow cool-weather pumpkin and butternut squashes, mushrooms, broccoli, and kale to shine in stews, chilis, and pasta dishes. Include root vegetables, such as turnips, parsnips, potatoes, carrots, and beets in your cooking as well.

winter Use hearty winter vegetables like cauliflower, cabbage, broccoli rabe, and sweet potatoes. To balance meals, serve with crisp salads featuring Belgian endive (chicory/witloof), fennel, and radicchio.

round it out

Once you have decided what dish to make as the centerpiece of your meal, choose from among a wide variety of appealing side dishes to round out the menu. Keep in mind both speed and ease of preparation.

steamed rice Of the many types of rice available, the long-grain varieties generally make the best side dishes. Aromatic basmati rice and jasmine rice are especially delicious with Asian dishes. For added flavor, cook rice in chicken broth instead of water, and stir chopped parsley or cilantro (fresh coriander) into the cooked rice.

couscous This North African dried semolina pasta, which looks like tiny grains, is widely available in instant form. It only needs a quick rehydrating in boiling water or broth before serving. If you wish, add chopped nuts, dried currants, or chopped mint.

roasted potatoes Cut small new potatoes in half and toss with olive oil. Spread in a single layer on a rimmed baking sheet, and roast at 425°F (220°C) until browned and tender, about 30 minutes. Season with salt and pepper and serve. For extra flavor, toss with minced garlic or chopped fresh rosemary before roasting.

artisanal bread Crusty, chewy bread is just the thing to accompany soup or stew. Heat it briefly in the oven, then slice and serve in a napkin-lined basket with softened butter or extra-virgin olive oil.

corn bread Warm slices of store-bought corn bread in the oven or toaster oven. Or, make your own using a mix or from scratch; add frozen corn kernels for texture and flavor. Serve alongside soups, chowders, or chilis.

tomatoes Flavorful in-season tomatoes go well with grilled fish and meats. Arrange the tomatoes on a platter, drizzle with olive oil, and season with salt and pepper. If desired, top with crumbled feta cheese.

sautéed baby spinach Packaged baby spinach can be quickly cooked as a side dish to grilled meats and seafood. Rinse the spinach and shake off excess water, but do not dry. Heat a little olive oil in a frying pan over medium heat (add a sliced garlic clove, if you like). Stir in the spinach, a big handful at a time, and cook just until all of the spinach has wilted. Season with salt and pepper and serve hot.

grilled vegetables When grilling fish or chops on one side of the grill as a main course, use the other side of the grill to cook an accompaniment. Grill asparagus whole; cut eggplant (aubergine) or zucchini (courgettes) lengthwise into slices about ½ inch (12 mm) thick. Brush the vegetables with olive oil and grill until tender. Season the vegetables with salt and pepper, and serve hot or at room temperature.

salad Purchase prewashed greens to save prep time, but always rinse and spin them dry before serving. Choose salad ingredients that harmonize with your meal: a mixture of spring greens with balsamic vinaigrette will go well with manicotti (page 76), while the all-American flavors of romaine hearts with a creamy ranch dressing will complement Cajun stew (page 43). Serve store-bought slaw, pasta salad, or potato salad alongside sandwiches.

easy desserts Serve seasonal fresh fruit drizzled with honey, cream, or yogurt; ice cream topped with nuts and warm chocolate sauce, caramel sauce, or hot espresso; or a selection of cheeses, served with sliced apples, dried fruit, and walnuts.

sample meals

These menus are designed to help you strategize your weekly meals. IN MINUTES menus highlight recipes that go together quickly and easily, while WEEKEND suppers require more cooking time. FIT FOR COMPANY features full menus that are perfect for both informal gatherings and festive occassions.

IN MINUTES	WEEKEND	FIT FOR COMPANY

IN MINUTES

Fontina, Ham & Pesto Panini
(page 14)

Sliced tomatoes with balsamic
vinegar & olive oil

**Penne with Winter Squash
& Pancetta**
(page 92)

Toasted baguette slices

Chicken Chili with Beans
(page 84)

Romaine (cos) lettuce
with herbed vinaigrette

Corn bread

**Grilled Pork Chops
with Romesco**
(page 26)

Green beans sautéed with shallots

Cheddar-Herb Biscuits
(page 40)

Roasted chicken sausages
& zucchini (courgettes)

WEEKEND

Baked Ham with Green Beans
(page 60)

Scalloped potatoes

Cheddar-Herb Biscuits (page 40)

Beef Salad with Mango
(page 68)

Sliced cucumbers
with rice vinegar

Steamed jasmine rice

Salt & Pepper Chicken
(page 54)

Sautéed asparagus with tarragon

Mashed potatoes

**Ziti with Arugula Pesto
& Chicken**
(page 10)

Grilled zucchini

Toasted garlic bread

Bacon & Egg Biscuits
(page 44)

Roasted potatoes with olive oil
and rosemary

Fruit salad

FIT FOR COMPANY

Three-Cheese Manicotti
(page 76)

Mixed greens with
balsamic vinaigrette

Lemon sorbet with fresh berries

Classic Crab Cakes
(page 80)

Shaved fennel and cabbage salad
with lemon vinaigrette

Fresh raspberry tart

Mushroom Tart
(page 34)

Watercress and Parmesan salad
with sherry vinaigrette

Strawberries with mascarpone
and brown sugar

Pappardelle with Ham & Peas
(page 67)

Roasted asparagus

Garlic crostini

Vanilla ice cream with caramel
sauce and toasted pecans

Prep ahead. Make a habit of prepping your ingredients the night before, whether it's chopping vegetables, rinsing salad greens, or cubing meat. Store ingredients in airtight containers in the refrigerator until needed.

Use the right tools. You don't need a lot of fancy equipment to prepare a good dinner. Good knives are indispensable to working efficiently in the kitchen. Start with an 8-inch (20-cm) chef's knife, a paring knife, a bread knife, and a knife sharpener. You also need a frying pan, a roasting pan with a rack, and a few heavy-bottomed saucepans in an assortment of sizes.

Ready your ingredients. When you start a recipe, take out and measure all your ingredients. That way, you won't find yourself digging through the pantry in search of sesame seeds or cider vinegar at the last minute, and counters won't be cluttered with cartons and jars. Pick up a set of small bowls in graduated sizes for holding the ingredients.

Clean as you go. Keep your kitchen organized by cleaning up as you go. Start out with a clean kitchen and an empty dishwasher—and make sure you have clean dish towels on hand. Put away ingredients as you use them, wipe down your work surfaces frequently, and move used pans and bowls to the sink or dishwasher once you are done with them. Fill dirty pans with hot water to soak while you're eating; by the time you're back in the kitchen, any browned-on food will be easier to scrub off.

shortcut ingredients

On days when you don't have time to cook a meal from scratch, well-stocked supermarkets and delicatessens offer lots of delicious, wholesome items to fill out your menu. Here are several ideas for lunch or dinner that you can put together at the last minute.

- **Rotisserie chicken** Buy enough chicken for two meals. On the first night, serve it accompanied with crusty bread and a simple salad. On another night, bone and skin the remaining chicken, shred the meat, and toss it with pasta and vegetables, or use it to make a chicken salad.

- **Cooked sausages** Keep fully cooked meat- or poultry-based sausages, such as chicken-apple, Italian, and kielbasa, in the refrigerator or freezer. Panfry the sausages until heated through and lightly browned, then slice lengthwise and serve with sautéed onions and peppers on warmed hero sandwich rolls or lengths of baguette.

- **Pasta** Always stock the pantry with a few packages of pasta and jars of pasta sauce. Add crumbled sausage meat or cubes of marinated baked tofu to the sauce for flavor and texture, or stir in leftover cooked greens, roasted red peppers (capsicums), and sliced olives. Top the sauced pasta with freshly grated Parmesan for a hearty supper.

- **Main-dish salads** Always keep prewashed packaged lettuce, mixed salad greens, or baby spinach in your refrigerator crisper. Rinse and dry quickly, toss with good-quality bottled salad dressing or a simple homemade vinaigrette, and top with canned tuna, olives, and sliced tomatoes or with sliced steak or chicken.

- **Pizza crust** Partially baked pizza crusts can be quickly transformed into a simple supper. Top with a prepared sauce, leftover vegetables, and grated cheese and bake in a 450°F (230°C) oven until the crust is heated through and the cheese is melted.

- **Pastry** Frozen pastry dough is an excellent alternative to making the pastry yourself. Thaw frozen pastry dough in the refrigerator according to the package instructions until ready to use.

shop smarter

Using good-quality, fresh ingredients will give you a head start toward great flavor and healthier eating. Look for a butcher, produce store, and market that you can rely on for first-rate goods and dependable service. Call ahead and place your order, so it's ready to pick up on your way home from work. Stop by your local farmers' market regularly for the freshest local produce and to keep up with what's in season.

■ **Produce** Look for locally grown produce whenever possible for better flavor and healthier eating. Items grown elsewhere have often been picked long before they ripen and rarely achieve peak flavor. Greens and herbs should be crisp and brightly colored, without dark edges or limp leaves. Root vegetables like carrots and beets should be hard, not bendable, and other vegetables, like cucumbers, eggplants (aubergines), and zucchini (courgettes), should be firm to the touch with taut skins. If you live near a regular farmers' market, get into the habit of visiting it once a week. You'll learn when specific items are in season, and you'll often find good deals on produce.

■ **Meat** Look for meat with bright, uniform color and no sign of shriveling at the edge. Fat should be bright white rather than grayish, and the meat should have a fresh smell. It's a good idea to ask your butcher to trim, grind, chop, or bone items as necessary, to save you time in the kitchen. Many butcher shops now carry organic and/or pasture-raised beef, pork, and lamb. Taste and compare what's offered to discover what tastes best to you. While much modern pork has been bred for leanness (often at the expense of moistness and tenderness), some specialty pork operations are returning to old-fashioned breeds whose meat can offer richer, more distinctive flavor. Ask your butcher if he or she carries pork from these heritage breeds.

■ **Poultry** Smooth skin, firm flesh, white to yellowish fat, and a fresh smell are the marks of quality poultry. A good butcher will be happy to cut up or debone a chicken or grind fresh turkey for you. Try cooking all of the different types of poultry available, such as kosher, organic, heritage breeds, and free range; and then buy what tastes best to you.

MAKE A SHOPPING LIST

prepare in advance Make a list of what you need to buy before you go shopping, and you'll save time.

make a template Create a list template, then fill it in during the week before you go shopping.

categorize your lists Use the following categories to keep your lists organized: pantry, fresh, and occasional.

■ **pantry items** Check the pantry and write down any items that need to be restocked to make the meals on your weekly plan.

■ **fresh ingredients** These are for immediate use and include produce, poultry, meats, and some cheeses. You may need to visit different stores or supermarket sections, so divide the list into subcategories, such as produce, dairy, and meats.

■ **occasional items** This is a list for refrigerated items that are replaced as needed, such as butter and eggs.

be flexible Be ready to change your menus based on the freshest ingredients at the market.

food processor This workhorse of the modern kitchen is good for chopping, grating, and shredding vegetables. A mini processor is useful for mincing a small amount of garlic or fresh herbs, while a standard model is handy for chopping onions, making pesto, and shredding cheese or carrots.

grill pan No time to fire up the grill? This heavy-bottomed, ridged pan is used on the stovetop and can yield seared, cross-hatched vegetables and meats that look and taste almost as if they were cooked on an outdoor grill. Always let the empty pan preheat over high heat for at least 5 minutes before adding the food.

salad spinner Wash and dry your greens using one handy implement. Whether your spinner uses a pump, crank, or pull cord, the centrifugal force whirling your greens will ensure a crisp, dry salad every time.

dried herbs Some dried herbs, including dried thyme, rosemary, and sage, can be used successfully when you don't have fresh herbs handy. Their flavor is more concentrated, however, so use only one-third to one-half the amount of fresh.

sharp knives You will prep your ingredients twice as fast if you don't have to struggle with a dull knife. It's a good idea to take a minute or two to sharpen a knife before you put it away, so it will be ready to use next time you cook.

make the most of your time

Once you've drawn up your weekly meal plan, you can begin thinking about how to make the most of your time. Get the shopping and prep work done in advance, and you'll be ready to cook when dinner time arrives.

- **Stock up.** Avoid last-minute shopping trips or missing ingredients by keeping your pantry well stocked. Make a note on your shopping list whenever you're getting low on any staple, and replace it promptly. Keep a good supply of basic nonperishable ingredients on hand. That way, you can improvise simple main and side dishes when needed.

- **Shop less.** Write out your shopping list as you plan your meals so you can pick up all the staples you'll need for the week in one trip. If you know that you'll be pressed for time during the week, purchase your meat and poultry along with your staples and wrap and freeze what you won't be using in the next couple of days.

- **Do it ahead.** Do as much as you can in advance when you have extra time. Wash, peel, and chop vegetables and store them in sealed plastic bags or airtight containers. Pound chicken or veal cutlets, wrap tightly with plastic wrap, and refrigerate. Prepare marinades or salad dressings and store in the refrigerator. Cook extra side dishes, such as rice, polenta, or steamed vegetables, and store in airtight containers until needed. Check your ingredients and tools the night before so you'll be able to find everything easily when you start to cook.

- **Double up.** Instead of serving a reheated version of the same dish the next night, double up the foundation of the meal. For example, roast two chickens or two pork tenderloins. Prepare one for tonight according to the recipe, and reserve the second for a hearty soup or salad the next night.

- **Cook smarter.** Read through the recipe from start to finish before you begin cooking. As you read, go through the recipe step by step in your mind and visualize all of the techniques. If you have friends or family around, figure out how they can help, whether it's peeling carrots, making a salad, or setting the table.

the well-stocked kitchen

Smart cooking is all about being prepared. Keeping your pantry, refrigerator, and freezer well stocked and organized means you'll save time when you are ready to cook a meal. And once you're in the habit of keeping track of the ingredients in your kitchen, you'll find that you can shop less frequently and spend less time in the store when you do.

On the pages that follow, you'll find an easy-to-use guide to all the ingredients needed to make the recipes in this book, along with dozens of tips on how to organize and store them properly. Check to see what's in your kitchen now, then all you have to do is make a list, go shopping, and fill your shelves. Once your kitchen is organized and stocked, you'll spend less time cooking and have more time to spend with your family and friends around the table.

the pantry

Typically, the pantry is a closet or one or more cupboards where you store canned and jarred foods, dried herbs and spices, oils and vinegars, grains and noodles, and such fresh foods as potatoes, onions, garlic, and shallots. Make sure that it is relatively cool, dry, and dark. It should also be a good distance from the stove, as heat can hasten spoilage.

stock your pantry

- Take inventory of what is in your pantry using the Pantry Staples list.

- Remove everything from the pantry; clean the shelves and reline with paper, if needed; and then resort the items by type.

- Discard items that have passed their expiration date or have a stale or otherwise questionable appearance.

- Make a list of items that you need to replace or stock.

- Shop for the items on your list.

- Restock the pantry, organizing items by type so everything is easy to find.

- Write the purchase date on perishable items and clearly label bulk items.

- Keep staples you use often toward the front of the pantry.

- Keep dried herbs and spices in their containers and preferably in a dedicated spice or herb organizer, shelf, or drawer.

keep it organized

- Look over the recipes in your weekly menu plan and check your pantry to make sure you have all the ingredients you'll need.

- Rotate items as you use them, moving the oldest ones to the front of the pantry so they will be used first.

- Keep a list of the items you use up so that you can replace them.

EQUIPMENT

An organized pantry works only if you have the right equipment, too. In Make It Easy on page 99, stovetop utensils are discussed. Here is the basic oven equipment.

baking dishes Use dishes that are attractive enough to go from the oven to the table. A shallow 9-by-13-inch (23-by-33-cm) dish and a deep 2½-qt (2.5 l) dish are versatile sizes.

roasting pans You'll want to cook enough meat or poultry to create leftovers for another meal. A 16-by-13-inch (40-by-33-cm) roasting pan will hold a large ham or six chicken breasts.

baking sheets Large, heavy-gauge rimmed baking sheets have many uses, from baking biscuits to roasting vegetables. It is handy to have two sheets so you can fill one while the other is in the oven.

tart pans Tarts, quiches, and tartlets baked in pans with removable bottoms can be unmolded for an attractive presentation. Have on hand a 9-inch (23-cm) tart pan and 4-inch (10-cm) tartlet pans.

PANTRY STORAGE

dried herbs & spices Dried herbs and spices start losing flavor after about 6 months. Buy them in small quantities, store in airtight containers labeled with the purchase date, and replace often.

oils Store unopened bottles of oil at room temperature in a cool, dark place. Oils will keep for up to 1 year, but their flavor diminishes over time. Store opened bottles for 3 months at room temperature or in the refrigerator for up to 6 months.

grains & pasta Store grains in airtight containers for up to 3 months, checking occasionally for signs of rancidity or infestation. The shelf life of most dried pastas is 1 year. Although they are safe to eat beyond that time, they will have lost flavor and might be brittle. Once you open a package, put the pasta you don't cook into an airtight container.

fresh pantry foods Store your fresh pantry items—garlic, onions, and some roots and tubers—in a cool, dark place, check them occasionally for sprouting or spoilage, and discard if necessary. Never store potatoes next to onions; when placed next to each other, they produce gases that hasten spoilage. Store citrus fruits and tomatoes uncrowded and uncovered on a countertop.

canned foods Discard canned foods if the can shows any signs of expansion or buckling. Once you have opened a can, transfer any unused portion to an airtight container or resealable plastic bag and refrigerate or freeze.

PANTRY STAPLES

GRAINS, PASTAS, & LEGUMES

black beans

cannellini or other small white beans

corn tortillas

couscous

dried pasta

lentils

long-grain rice

quick-cooking polenta

FRESH FOODS

garlic

ginger

lemons

limes

onions

oranges

plum (Roma) tomatoes

potatoes

red bell peppers (capsicums)

SPIRITS

dry white wine

full-bodied red wine

PACKAGED FOODS

Asian fish sauce

broth (beef, chicken, vegetable)

canned plum (Roma) tomatoes, whole and chopped

coconut milk

dried bread crumbs

Japanese bread crumbs (*panko*)

roasted red bell peppers (capsicums)

Thai red curry paste

tomato paste

Worcestershire sauce

OILS & VINEGARS

Asian sesame oil

balsamic vinegar

olive oil

red wine vinegar

rice vinegar

sherry vinegar

DRIED HERBS & SPICES

black peppercorns

Cajun seasoning

cayenne pepper

chili powder

dry mustard

oregano

paprika, sweet and smoked

red pepper flakes

sage

sesame seeds

thyme

MISCELLANEOUS

bittersweet chocolate

baking powder

cornstarch (cornflour)

flour, (plain) all-purpose

light brown sugar

powdered (icing) sugar

the refrigerator & freezer

Once you have stocked and organized your pantry, you can apply the same time-saving principles to your refrigerator and freezer. The refrigerator is ideal for keeping your meats, poultry, vegetables, and leftovers fresh for a relatively short time. The freezer will preserve most of the flavor and nutrients in braises, stews, and soups for up to a few months if carefully packaged in airtight containers.

general tips

- Foods lose flavor under refrigeration, so proper storage and an even temperature of below 40°F (5°C) is important.

- Freeze foods at 0°F (-18°C) or below to retain color, texture, and flavor.

- Don't crowd foods in the refrigerator or freezer. Air should circulate freely to keep foods evenly cooled.

- To prevent freezer burn, use only moistureproof wrappings, such as aluminum foil, airtight plastic containers, or resealable plastic bags.

- Some items, such as crab cakes and biscuits, should be frozen individually and then stored. Freeze, uncovered, on baking sheets until firm, then wrap each item in plastic wrap and pack them in heavy-duty resealable plastic bags.

leftover storage

- Most prepared dishes can be stored in the refrigerator for up to 3 days or in the freezer for up to 3 months.

- Check the contents of the refrigerator at least once a week and promptly discard old or spoiled food.

- Let food cool to room temperature before refrigerating or freezing. Transfer the cooled food to an airtight plastic or glass container, leaving room for expansion if freezing. Or, cut the cooled food into a resealable plastic freezer bag, expelling as much air as possible before sealing.

REHEATING MEALS

When reheating refrigerated or frozen leftovers in the oven, reheat at the original cooking temperature, and never use a higher temperature or you could have dry, overcooked results.

Always use a preheated oven for reheating. Do not transfer frozen food in a ceramic or glass baking dish directly from the freezer unless the oven is preheated or it could break.

If using a microwave to reheat, use Medium power. If reheated on High power, the edges could overcook before the center is heated.

THAWING FROZEN FOODS

in the refrigerator Place the food in the refrigerator for at least 8 hours or up to overnight. By using this method, you will preserve the taste, color, and texture of the food.

in the microwave Place the food in the microwave and heat on Low power or the defrost setting. Reheat or cook the food immediately after thawing.

fresh herb & vegetable storage

■ Trim the stem ends of a bunch of parsley, stand the bunch in a glass of water, drape a plastic bag loosely over the leaves, and refrigerate. Wrap other fresh herbs in a damp paper towel, slip into a plastic bag, and store in the crisper. Rinse and stem all herbs just before using.

■ Store tomatoes and eggplants (aubergines) at room temperature.

■ Cut about ½ inch (12 mm) off the end of each asparagus spear; stand the spears, tips up, in a glass of cold water; and refrigerate, changing the water daily. The asparagus will keep for up to 1 week.

■ Rinse leafy greens, such as kale, spin dry in a salad spinner, wrap in damp paper towels, and store in a resealable plastic bag in the crisper for up to 1 week. In general, store other vegetables in resealable bags in the crisper and rinse before using. Sturdy vegetables will keep for up to a week; more delicate ones will keep for only a few days.

meat & poultry storage

■ Use fresh meat and poultry within 2 days of purchase. If buying packaged meats, check the expiration date and use before that date.

■ Place packaged meats on a plate in the coldest part of the refrigerator. If only part of a package is used, discard the original wrapping and rewrap in fresh wrapping.

cheese & dairy storage

■ Wrap all cheeses well to prevent them from drying out. Hard cheeses, such as Parmesan, have a low moisture content, so they keep longer than fresh cheeses, such as mozzarella and ricotta. Store soft and semisoft cheeses, such as Fontina, for up to 2 weeks and hard cheeses for up to 1 month.

■ It is best to store dairy products in their original packaging. Check the expiration date and use before that date.

index

weldon**owen**

415 Jackson Street, Suite 200, San Francisco, CA 94111
www.wopublishing.com

MEALS IN MINUTES SERIES

Conceived and produced by Weldon Owen Inc.

Copyright © 2008 by Weldon Owen Inc. and Williams-Sonoma, Inc.

The recipes in this book have been previously published as *Make Ahead* in the Food Made Fast series.

Printed by 1010 Printing in China

Set in Formata
This edition first printed in 2011
10 9 8 7 6 5 4 3 2 1

Library of Congress Cataloging-in-Publication data is available.

Weldon Owen is a division of
BONNIER

Photographer Bill Bettencourt
Food Stylist Kevin Crafts
Photographer's Assistants Angelica Cao
Food Stylist's Assistants Alexa Hyman
Text Writer Rick Rodgers

ACKNOWLEDGMENTS

Weldon Owen wishes to thank the following people for their generous support in producing this book: Heather Belt, Ken DellaPenta, Lesli Neilson, and Sharon Silva.

ISBN-13: 978-1-61628-257-8
ISBN-10: 1-61628-257-6

A NOTE ON WEIGHTS AND MEASURES

All recipes include customary U.S. and metric measurements. Metric conversions are based on a standard developed for these books and have been rounded off. Actual weights may vary.